HARPOON

JOSHUA
ROBERT
LONG

ISBN: 978-1-105-87519-9

HARPOON is a production of a man with a cherry-red fence and The Polkadodge Organization. **HARPOON** is printed and distributed on behalf of a man with a cherry-red fence and The Polkadodge Organization by Lulu, Incorporated of Raleigh, North Carolina.

More information on The Polkadodge Organization can be found by visiting the organization's website: polkadodge.org

More information on the man with the cherry-red fence is available upon request by visiting the author's website: joshuarobertlong.com

Some of these works have appeared in various forms in the following places: The Polkadodge Organization website, the author's own website, and in other spaces/blogs throughout the internet.

This book was compiled from several chapbooks prior to his (mediocre) success, and from varied scribbled notes found around his house.

HARPOON was edited, constructed, and designed by The Legal Endowment For Wednesday Night Activities. The cover design was done by Robert High.

HARPOON

CONTENTS:

AN ORDER OF THANKS, IN NO PARTICULAR ORDER

Madeline McGraw. Krysta, Charles, Jeremy, Tara, Alexis, & Taylor Long. Jennifer, Jim, & Dominic Fazio. Robert & Phyllis Bayman. Martin Harold Benedict Borchers. Justin David Koontz. Touria Tougui. Alex Callanan. Yosef Johnson. Michael Penney. Whoever worked at Subway on Covington Avenue in the early 2000s. Casey Filmer. Tyler Hurwitz. Randy Conner. Matthew Mandville. Rennie's Mill River Road and that strange sort of park that somehow connects itself with it.

"Night"

the girl walks by
the counter, grabbing
the filled-in ashtrays.

I have no time to think
anymore
as she goes by.

the lights in this place
seem so mad,
cherry-red,
oh-my-god, etc.

the best of us rip it off
of each other.

we glance in all directions
as if taking in something
for the steal.

we no longer know
what it is anymore
we're looking for.

and having said that,
the ashtray returns.

“Modern Wage”

I find myself trying hard
at life.

in the mornings I look
at myself in the mirror

each time touching
the lines of time
as the sands brush
off the skin

enough time has passed
now to build mountains

not enough hourly
to smile
on the way
out the door.

"Momentary Hook"

quote me on this one:

landslides
victories
little victories

the fish is happiest
when he finds himself
in the bottle
of the barrel.

and in both
this and that

I swim.

naked.

ambient.

sideways.

"Harpoon"

the harpoon is a tool
best saved for
failure eyes

we all have our moments
in these seas

catching breath
leads to diving
down to
another

we're all the right type
of cold
as the clouds
settle down
overhead.

"Like a Rodent"

there's a rodent in
my heart
and she's calamity

there are skin-tears
on her claws
and it's enough
to bring on the sweat

I'm apparent of my failures
shortcomings, etc

I blare them on the highway
like the radio's Chevrolet

and in those times
when the dial can't
be heard over the wind
coming in through the floorboards

the calm
comes up my throat
and the claws
hold less
into the skin.

"Heartbreak Hotel"

as the twilight
hits the living room
and the light
in the corner
begins to display

we're looking more
like each other now
we're looking more
older

we begin in the middle
like bread
and mold

we force ourselves onto
each other and tell
the same stories again

there is a rhythm
to it, I haven't quite
solved it.

"12:08:43 AM"

hearts
are made of
metal

future-tense

eventually then
made of metal

we'll trade our
spoons
in
for better
valves

things to
do the pumping.

“12:13:34 AM”

I saw Jesse the other day
she seemed
happier
than the last time

I think the curve-balls
eventually stop
meaning so much
when you just lay
down and
let time
defeat you.

"12:16:03 AM"

we are
hearts

beating
bleeding
winning

we are life
personified
personalized

we let the webbing
undo itself

we lack the
printer ink
to tell the world
our true feelings.

"12:17:46 AM"

we the people
just want
answers

we want
honest handshakes

we spend our whole
lives
actually getting
very few
of those.

"Shelf Life"

beat the fox
with the bag
of shells
each
crunch
cracks
and
shoulders
another
burden
to feel the pain
through

the fox
only knows
how to take
it
how to lay down
and take it
like a Saturday
night
friend

we're not
bought
and sold
anymore
we're already
back
for sale again.

"Winter Gone Spring"

remember, remember
the 24th of February

it's cold
and warm
snow
ice
rain
fury
to the wind
fury to the
choice
that
WE MADE IT
THIS WAY.

no liberty here,
no heart
in the rear-view

it's all highway
out here
babe,

we're no longer
asphalt
to the pages
of history

"Butter Nose"

earlier
tonight
she ate my nose

no butter
or salt
or fork
just bit
aggressive
both
passive
and forward
open & honest
in line
for sandwiches

one probably observed
me as a man
abused
as a man in time
for the hurricane
and outside
the flags
on the poles
all seem
ready to ricochet

maybe tonight's the night
we're not here
anymore

let the buzzer ring
let the buzzer sing
OH SAY CAN YOU SEE?

surely, she can't

"Favor"

the odds
not in favor

no more favors
no more sock drawers
no more lettuce-washing
no more tomatoes
on the vines

the vines are all
much like
rubber to pull apart

and now the horses
all pull apart
they're made of rubber
themselves

elastic they go
stretching
like sidewalks

the sidewalks
never know
anymore
the pace of our
footsteps

we're ghosts in
our own
world

we dream the light
of night
in the satisfaction
of morning.

"Talking to the old friend, Sii"

looked to Sii
for answers

never had any

putting the teacup
down

there were
rings of
water all tracked
in tracks
around the table

hello heart,
have you got the co-pay?

there's no play for you
here without the co-pay.

how much now can we offer you?
we need to offer
you much more

I turn back to Sii
to see he's still there
shaved head
heart inside
his lover long gone
and I hold
his hand
trying to take myself
inside his heart

try to take my opportunity
to understand

whatever sense of emotion
is left in there
to convey
for the outside
sets of eyes

"Melatonin"

demons
in my nightstand
they recollect
the men
who've shared
my space

there were women
too,
but they seem insignificant
because
they all
leave

so do the women
so do the men

nowadays
we're poor
lonely
can't afford
even the tobacco

we're empty
like faucets
dripping
through
a calcium-tinged
water

molecules
begin
building crystals
the Articulates
now
are laughing

at the notion
of being “calcium-tinged”

"Tomorrow We'll Be Quicker"

we're modern

post-modern
wasn't real

we're as modern
as the changing
of the television

the guard has changed
hearts all changed

the cats won't leave the items
on my table alone

we're alone
and we're cold
and we always thought
that love with another
would carry us through the night

here now
here is what we have found:
it's mostly true
but it's mostly still
up in the air

how do you put faith in something
when everyone else
puts the same faith in you?

I look at her and see that
it's all a matter of absolute failing
unless I sit here and try

and I will always try

there's not much left beyond
her if she chose to leave

it would be much easier in that
situation to just sign a waiver.

"Headquarters"

I was going to
remove
its body and engine

put it inside of you
but you wouldn't open
your legs
you left me in
a
sort of blue-pill-shaded
hole

I don't even remember sleep
though

there was a morning-after
awakened
to the prospect
of the blood of
the 5W30

there on my flesh
I rubbed it in

there was flesh to burn
and I planned on
burning it on you.

"Polkadotted Type"

Sally
would take
water
and die

across the southern
tips
northern tips

Sally would die
Sally gave heart
to the cause
of miles

highway miles
and highway
roadsigns

all the way
all the way

they came
and went

"When You Say You Need Me Tonight"

the car
had beautiful
eyes

rolling across
the hills

down outside
the valley
beneath
the crust
and beyond
the edge of
the dust

circular motions
evaporate
there

circular motions
read and head
themselves
in the bush

"Toss the Glass"

before
lights
there was
light
which was still
before darkness
on the edge
of the toast

burning
smells in the morning
all recollect
the times before
when it was more
or less
just the flicker
of the flame
which led to the night

now
as
it stands
I'm only standing around
shining up the armor
waiting on the knighthood

"Can't Keep Disguise in White"

we're maroon
in heart

the blood
pumps
in a purplish
pattern
inside
the walls

I've painted them
red
I've taken the time
to read
the words
buried within
the texture
of the strokes

the maroon has all
mended
into the wall

there is no space for
Frost in the pages
of my history

it's as mundane
as using the gas pump
in the middle of the summer

watching
the success of being
mediocre

“Make Sure You're Not Followed”

let us park down
by the coast
and soak into
the falling moon
rising again
days after morning
after morrow

where now is it
that we were going with this?

"Out of Crush"

harps play
the music
we hear
when the silence
runs over
our eyes

our necks
all swan-like
into the curtains
which are slowly-quickly
falling

the desert still shows
up
beneath the curtains

nothing known
knowing nothing

gains are made
gains are made the most of

"Even Out"

in weather like this
in scenery like this
we're born to die

we're born to die
without the rights
we searched out
in our youth

nothing more can be
made
but to know
we played the game
in a fair way

clouds will swirl
in light and dark
and blended
vanilla and chocolate

egg all over our face
one face
walking straight into
the fire

"Spit It Out Again"

what's a story without
an ending?

that story is before you
in the tips and heels
of your shoes

appearing more
when you take the chance
to walk beyond the grass
of your yard

and appearing more so
even after
if you choose
to stare back into the sun

so much effort put
into looking forward
yet
so little effort
put into looking back

"I Can Hear You Through The Window"

restaurants
all serve the same
food

all serve the same
exhausted
waiters and waitresses

and together at the table
with your peers
they are mocked

bean sprouts
on bread
cost less at home
but your heart has no desire
to support a local

searching from the bottom
to the top

we'll see
when the plates land

"Stuck on Puzzle"

we're doom
doom in a handbag

we all go
place to place

having a bit of
a laugh

nothing but romance now
in the eyes of the romantic

but how can we possibly be
romantic
in the fever of the evening?

she laid her eyes down
on me
down on my sides

sizing me up
sizing me down
only interested in
what goes on around
the corners of my head

and which head it is
is the true northern
one

possessing such thought
and creation
burning only gates
that exist
outside of Eden

"Fingers Dim The Lights"

smashing rumors
down
with hammers

fists of nails
all bringing
clarity
to the audience
eager
for fresh meat

the fresh meat is key
to their evenings in the
sand

their light beers
all taste like water

everything based on water
even the basis of my jeans

which finally feel a bit-less-than-snug
where does all the asphalt come from—that's what I wonder

as I face it myself
hands bound
rights being read
here and here again

"On The Back of The Backdrop"

never much left
to feed the children

she rides a high horse into
town and buys her groceries

the ones with stickers
that wash off beneath the
rush of the sink

the pan always burns
the stove burner
heating too hot

always
constant
perhaps an issue due to wiring
or gas-gauge settings

things beyond me

for I am only a man
with a desire to eat
and I own no horse
I am only a resonator

"Comfortable Shoes"

let us have a demonstration of your skills

this is what they ask of me
this is before they ask me why
I would possibly want a career in
sales

yesterday
was free

the day before that
was free

the day before the day before that
was free

and now it all suddenly
costs money?

nobody bothers to explain
the ambition
one should have
to motivate themselves
into selling themselves
for someone else

"Tomorrow I'll Be Faster"

to ponder
the blank space
ahead of me

to know
a puff or two on the cigarette
will clarify my point of view

false
starts
false promises

there is no inspiration
in the clouds
rolling around

the eyes
just fail

fail and wipe
the windows
down

the rain is bringing
about the steam
the hot and cold
contrast
between
the ins and the outs

“I Know The Way Back, If You Know The Way”

we're cold
we're cold

we want the gas
to be more
than the condensation
but we know
they're pals

they're horses
of the same
field

they graze
and no,
they don't graze

let us not get technical
in the eyes
of the audience

nor should it be
known
that if we turn around
they'll all be looking in
looking for
a way
to dice the thought

"Even If It's Rigged"

stop
the lines

hold
the presses

it's as reminiscent
as the cold
tea sitting
on the corner
of the table

and to heat it again
would take away

already now
I feel the burns
of the dull razor
dragging stripes
across my face

the shower
hasn't even started
though, trust in that,
it is close

all rubbish in the bin

"The Lord Telephone Part II"

Jesus is here

his hair
all the same
as the pictures contain

and his sandals
are broken in

slightly worn
yet still in style

the children
will copy him
in due time

when the seasons
demand it

we're supercharged
with hype
with hope
and animosity

never again though
will we look
at sandals
quite the same way

"Sunset Eyes"

the cigarette is done

down to the last
bit or flicker
of light

the ash is no longer
apparent

these cigarettes
don't yet require
fire

lungs are burning
the smooth vapor
nights are coming

the shower
has become
the next frontier

we're cold in the wind
yet there is no wind
inside these walls
insulation has become
the gift of the gods
we've never met

beneath me now
all the old clothes
all tomorrow's parties
and none of them will
be ready
to see what has become
of this cold, naked bag
of flesh

all covered and hair
and the past mistakes
and victories
one-in-the-same

"Satellite Songs"

we are more than
victory
when we let ourselves
free

the hardest part
of modern reality
is letting the world
understand
what "free" still means

we used to look west,
but now we just look
at ourselves

somewhere between
the desk & the horizon
an eye has already seen

and we know now
that we end up beyond
the heliosphere.

ABOUT THE AUTHOR

Joshua Robert Long received a BA in both English and Creative Writing from The Ohio State University in Columbus, Ohio. In the past he has authored numerous chapbooks and traditional books including: **TRANSLATING THE AVENUES**, **LEAVING FROST UPON THE WALLS**, and **RUMOR MIRROR.** In addition to that, he has also co-authored **MIXTAPE** and **MIXTAPE, VOLUME II: FROM YELLOW SPRINGS TO FLAGSTAFF** with Justin David Koontz. Joshua was born in Dayton, Ohio, has resided all over North America, & currently finds himself living in Yellow Springs, Ohio.

OTHER TITLES AVAILABLE

Translating The Avenues / Walleyed Press
Mixtape (With Justin David Koontz) / Walleyed Press
Leaving Frost Upon the Walls / LP
Mixtape, Vol. II (With Justin David Koontz) / Walleyed Press

www.ingramcontent.com/pod-product-compliance
Ingram Content Group UK Ltd.
Pitfield, Milton Keynes, MK11 3LW, UK
UKHW020231250726
13967UKWH00001B/306

9 781105 875199